All About Poetry

The Northern Counties

Edited by
Allison Jones

This book belongs to

First published in Great Britain in 2010 by

Remus House
Coltsfoot Drive
Peterborough
PE2 9JX
Telephone: 01733 890066
Website: www.youngwriters.co.uk

All Rights Reserved
Book Design by Spencer Hart
© Copyright Contributors 2010
SB ISBN 978-0-85739-221-3

Foreword

At Young Writers our defining aim is to promote an enjoyment of reading and writing amongst children and young adults. By giving aspiring poets the opportunity to see their work in print, their love of the written word as well as confidence in their own abilities has the chance to blossom.

Our latest competition *Poetry Express* was designed to introduce primary school children to the wonders of creative expression. They were given free reign to write on any theme and in any style, thus encouraging them to use and explore a variety of different poetic forms.

We are proud to present the resulting collection of regional anthologies which are an excellent showcase of young writing talent. With such a diverse range of entries received, the selection process was difficult yet very rewarding.

From comical rhymes to poignant verses, there is plenty to entertain and inspire within these pages. We hope you agree that this collection bursting with imagination is one to treasure.

Contents

Nick Glen (11) 1
Jordan Blaney (10) 1
Callum Harkin (9) 2
Owen Colligan (8) 2
Umer Memon (10) 3
William Dingwall (10) 3
Mackenzie Helme (5) 4
Conner Appleyard (7) 4
Emily Georgeson (5) 4
Lauren Johnson (5) 5
Shannon Knox (7) 5

Balshaw Lane Primary School, Euxton
Josh Harrison (11) 5
Ellie McManus (10) 6
Conor Hughes (11) 7
Holly Webster (10) 8
Lydia Brooks (10) 9
Sam Moore (9) 10
Jessica Elizabeth Nelson (11) 11
Daniel Haselden (10) 12
Rachel Tincello (11) 12
Thomas Holmes (10) 13
Ellis Hawkins (11) 13
Emelia Rose Carter (10) 14
Nikkita Kaur Birk (11) 15
Charlotte Walsh (10) 16
Charlotte Bradbury (11) 17
Kirsty Pope (10) 18
Brandon Moseley (10) 18
Harvey Unsworth (11) 19
Melissa McGhee (9) 19
Joshua Bergin (11) 20

Bentley High Street Primary School, Bentley
Ebony Taylor (10) 20
Julieanne Wootton (11) 21
Jordan Hendry (11) 21
Michael Glassner Leadenham (10) 22
Lewis Gilbert (10) 23

Bethany Copestake (11) 23
Kyle Cordon (10) 24
Jasmine Lailey (9) 24
Lochlan Cunningham (8) 25
Kris Pickard (11) 25
Liam Pidcock (10) 26
Jennifer Field (11) 26
Olivia Olsen (9) 27
Rebecca Vickers (9) 27
Bethany Baugh (10) 28
Jack Livingstone (9) 28
Chloe Horsfield (10) 29
Chloe Powell (9) 29
Sophie Jane Coy (8) 30
Nicolette Marsh (11) 30
Luke Jackson (8) 31
Liam Macey (9) 31
Charlie Leek (11) 32
Josh Maddison (11) 32
Megan Louise Todd (11) 33
Coralena Ann Dear (10) 33
Elliot Sprakes (8) 33
Mason Owen (11) 34
Courtney Shaw (11) 34
Charlotte Parkes (8) 34
Liam Wortley (9) 35
Spiderlouise Williams (8) 35
Kirra Nimmo (9) 35
Joe Benson (11) 36
McKenzie Baker-Ward (8) 36
Michael Robert Cooper (8) 36
Morgan Newton (9) 37
Samuel Bowker (8) 37
Marlie Rodney (10) 37
Joshua James Vidler (10) 38
Harrison Stephens (10) 38
Chloe Jade Read (8) 38

Birdwell Primary School, Birdwell
Olivia Cawthorn (11) 39

Fulwood & Cadley CP School, Fulwood
Mia Taylor (8) 39
Laura Jackson (10) 40
Dilan Vadher (11) 41
James Nicolas Bracken (10) 42
Vishal Gohil (11) 43
Jay Bond (11) 44
Lydia Dixon 44
Hassan Bakhat (8) 45
Khalil Patel (8) 45
Megan Haigh (10) 46
Katharine Beavers (11) 46
Conor Lambert (11) 47
Arooj Ali (9) 47
Adam Culcman (10) 40
Joe Hyde (11) 48
Christopher Dewhurst (11) 49
Poppy Wigg (11) 49
Calista Gibirdi (10) 50
Adam Stuart Wilkinson (11) 50
Yasser Karim Khan (8) 51
Lorna Clitheroe (8) 51
Jade Preston (10) 52

Linton-on-Ouse Primary School, Linton-on-Ouse
Emily Garner (10) 52
Jessica Luck (11) 53
Miles Manfield (11) 53
Robert Garner (10) 54
Conor Aston (10) 54
Amelia Brown (10) 55
Bethany McClelland (11) 55
Harry Mannion (9) 55

Out Rawcliffe CE School, Out Rawcliffe
John Bonsall (10) 56
John Robert Davies (11) 57
Kimberley Jane Newhouse (9) 58
Anna Jenkinson (9) 59
James Guthrie (10) 60
Eve MacMillan (8) 60
William Lewis (10) 61
Anna Charles (9) 62
Joshua Philip Kelsall (9) 62
Alex Wallace (8) 63

St Francis of Assisi Catholic Primary School, Skelmersdale
Harri Kildear 63
Lauren May Shields (11) 64
Elisha Lyon 65
Darbie Barlow (11) 66
Wiktoria Gerka (11) 67
Saffron Ryan 68
Callum Morgan Gary Henwood (11) 69
Zoe Livesey (11) 70
Chris Haworth (10) 71
Lucy Hume (11) 72
Liam Austin 73
Thomas Wise (11) 74
Liam Murray 75

St Paul's CE Primary School, Stalybridge
Gareth Smith (11) 75
Rhiannon Stephenson (10) 76
Robbie Scott Hunter (11) 77
Emma Louise Scanlan (11) 78
Devon Bellamy & Luke Chisnall (10) 78
George Smith (11) 79
Bethany Bailey (11) 79
Ellie Goodyear (11) 80

St William's RC (VA) Primary School, Trimdon
Sarah Murray (9) 80
Blaize Marshall (10) 81
Natalie Bastiman (10) 82
William Reid (11) 83
Dominic Howarth (8) 84
Lydia Sheldon (9) 84
Shannon Louise Teresa Ferry (10) 85
Rebecca Elizabeth Dobson (10) 85
Ethan Josef Mould (11) 86
Daniel Bastiman (9) 86
Lauren Easton (11) 87
Ben Merrington (9) 87
Katie Spellman (9) 88
Eavie Proffitt (9) 88
Lucy Tate (9) 89
Callum Atkinson (9) 89
Jade Oakes (10) 90
Jack Foote (9) 90
Eddie Reid (9) 91

Aleysha Oakes (10) 91

Spennithorne CE Primary School, Spennithorne
Jake Fishburn (9) 92
Jamie Harrington (8) 92
Lauren Fall (9) 93
Maggie Manning (9) 94
Tom Partridge (9) 95
Emily Wilson (8) 95
Jack Harry Tait (9) 96
George Leathley (9) 96
Bethany Harrington (8) 97
Olivia Eyre (7) 97
Ruth Metcalfe (9) 98
Matthew Heinze (9) 98
William Cooper (8) 99

Stradbroke Primary School, Sheffield
Lewis Moorcroft (10) 99
Isobel Vaughan (10) 100
Aaron Shaw & Connor Walsh (10) 100
Libby Hines (10) 101
Olivia Clarke (9) 101
Charlie Bower (10) 102
Joshua Kelly (9) 102
Ebony Wilson, Amber Bowie (10)
& Adam Marples (9) 103
Holly Liversidge
& Georgia Greaves (10) 103
Lucy Birch (10) & Kady Shepley (9) ... 104
Charlotte Mellor (10) 104
Maisie Marriott (8) 105
Joshua Hirst & Corben Timms (10).... 105
Curtis Emmingham (8) 105
Alicia Beniston (7) 106
Leighann Sharpe
& Natalie Hawkins (10) 106
Jayden Lee Moat (10) 106
Adam Holmshaw (8) 107
Shelby Emmingham (10) 107
Abbigail Beniston
& Andrew Gregory (10) 107
Kelsey Bellamy (7) 108
Caiden Smith (7) 108
Paige Pickering (7) 108
Kathryn Robinson (8) 109

Georgia Johnston (8) 109
Tommy Cooke (8) 109
Georgie Samantha Jackson (10) 110
Kyle Joseph Haig (8) 110

The Park Primary School, Runcorn
Richard Michael Ireland (8) 110
Lee May (8) 111

Walsden St Peter's CE Primary School, Todmorden
Alice Routledge (11) 111
Amy Cupac (11) 112
Jack Cryer (11) 112
Sara Power (10) 113
Adam Georgiou (10) 113
Ria Montgomery (11) 114
Joe Wright (11) 114
Katie Skowron (11) 115
Rhys Moores (10) 115
Josh Hird (10) 116

Woodhouse Community Primary School, Bishop Auckland
Brydon Kenney (9) 116
Kamran Howard (8) 117
Bethany Smirthwaite (10) 117
Sean McGrady (8) 118
Aaron Bailey (10) 118
Courtney Louise Hopps (11) 119
Ashley Cumberland (10) 119
Chloe Pattison (8) 120
Lee Anderson (11) 120
Kieran Pattison (9) 121

The Poems

My Cat

My cat is a fussy feline,
I doubt she even thinks that she's mine.
With her nose in the air
She says, 'Stroke if you dare.'

Sat on the mat she's waiting for me.
Oh, no she's not, she just wants her tea.
But when it's time for me to eat
She thinks it's her very own little treat!

Her coat shiny black, from all her preening,
She lies in the sun, purring and dreaming,
Probably of being worth a million dollars.
Oh why did we buy her that diamond cat collar?

She walks round like she's queen bee,
But it's not her fault, I spoiled her you see.
And here she comes now, a welcome sight,
To curl up next to me all through the night.

Nick Glen (11)

Pollution On Earth

In spring I would like the factories to stop polluting the air
And people to plant trees, giving oxygen
In summer I would like gangs to stop dumping stuff in the river
In autumn I would like people to stop capturing animals
And setting lots of traps
In winter I would like the environment not to become so cold
Because elderly people really suffer and become very ill.

Jordan Blaney (10)

Colours Of The Whole Wide World

Red is like the colour of a bright red apple, a nice red fox
White is the colour of the lovely night-time moon
And the whiteboard in this very room
Yellow is the colour of the sun in the day
Yellow is the colour of butter on jacket potatoes
Green is the colour of the forest leaves
And the colour of grass
Blue is the colour of the lovely sea
And a couple of nice blue books
Purple is the colour of a big, ripe, juicy plum, just been picked.

Callum Harkin (9)

Dangerous Eagle

Eagles look furious and dangerous with mean eyes,
Eagles sound like a dragon about to attack you,
Eagles feel soft and fluffy,
Eagles act as though they are going to kill you,
Eagles are an endangered species,
Eagles smell of fish that they have caught from the river,
Eagles like to dive into the river and eat the fish,
Eagles have razor-sharp talons,
Eagles hate hunters shooting them down,
Eagles are fierce predators,
Eagles love eating the lovely fish.

Owen Colligan (8)

Colours

Brown reminds me of trees in autumn, fluttering in the breeze.
Blue reminds me of the sea in the distance.
Red reminds me of a rose like my mum.
Black reminds me of ghosts in the dark.

Green reminds me of the rainforest in the Amazon.
White reminds me of a snowman in winter.
Silver reminds me of a shield in the war.
Orange reminds me of the oranges I eat.

Pink reminds me of my sister because she likes pink.
Gold reminds me of the crown the Queen wears.
Yellow reminds me of the sun on a nice day.
My favourite colour is red because my mum likes red.

Umer Memon (10)

The Needy Shoe

I live on a human
And I'm usually with my twin,
My arms always get knotted around my stiff neck
And I can't move without my friend, the man.

I see everything from my hundreds of tiny eyes,
Sometimes I feel sick because I'm going up and down off the ground,
Most times I'm sad because I'm left in the cupboard
But I'm a bit happy because I'm still with my twin.

William Dingwall (10)

Untitled

She crawls like a baby,
She's fast like an ostrich,
She fights like a lion,
She falls off ladders,
She is bigger than a monster,
She is my sister.

Mackenzie Helme (5)

Daffodils

When I see the golden daffodils
It fills my heart with glee.

As all the daffodils I see
Sprightly, up and down in the sun.

My heart has never had so much pleasure before.

Conner Appleyard (7)

My Dog

She is as fluffy as a bear,
She is as white as a piece of paper,
She is as hungry as a hippo,
She is as beautiful as a butterfly,
She is my dog.

Emily Georgeson (5)

What Am I?

I am spiky
You can hear the sea
You can find me on the beach
What am I?
A shell!

Lauren Johnson (5)

Who Is She?

She is as fluffy as a woolly jumper
She runs as fast as a cat
She is as kind as a book
She eats as much as a cheetah
She's as playful as a child
She has teeth as strong as a door trap
She is my dog, Ellie.

Shannon Knox (7)

The Waterfall

The sun beams down onto the spectacular water,
Which gushes down from the top of the waterfall.
Bombs of water hit the rocks below, eroding away,
Because of the water crashing into them.
Water below flows effortlessly, like a bike rolling down a hill,
Swiftly the water drags the rubble down the waterfall
And into the deep end of the bubbly plunge pool.

Josh Harrison (11)
Balshaw Lane Primary School, Euxton

The Wonderful Waterfall

Spectacular and extraordinary
The waterfall gushes down
And hits the water below
With an almighty splash!

Then it thunders down
Twirling and splashing
Whilst eating away the rock
At the sides and underneath.

Gradually making the river deeper and wider
More room for the powerful water to move.

Gleaming on the waterfall
The sun makes the water sparkle
Showing its true beautiful
Deep blue.

When the waterfall hits the river
It's like cars crashing fiercely
And reacting quickly
In the water's case, the spray
Fills the air.

Day and night it never stops
Gushing over the slippy rocks.

The bubbles at the bottom
Make it like a hot tub
With mountains of froth piling high
White as snow.

If it's too much to ask
Next time you pass . . .
Please take a look
At my intrinsic beauty.

Ellie McManus (10)
Balshaw Lane Primary School, Euxton

The Waterfall

The gushing waterfall crashing down
Into the foamy pool beneath
Roaring with laughter
The thunderous waterfall smashes
Against the rocks
Eroding them
As if to make them into piercing daggers.

The sound of twirling torrents
Thunders in the air
Pounding the ears of creatures
Nearby
Beaming sunlight glistens
On the stampede of powerful water
Spray bursts out of the waterfall
Like dancing fireworks.

Bashing and thrashing
Water rapidly gushes down
Hitting and splitting the rocks on its way
Huge amounts of water race down
Destroying anything in its path
Unstoppable!

Suddenly, calm; still; slow
As its fierce, ferocious fight with the rocks
Comes to an end
The only thing heard is the pitter-patter of droplets
Falling from the defeated rocks.

Conor Hughes (11)
Balshaw Lane Primary School, Euxton

Commotion In The Ocean

There's a commotion in the ocean,
As water runs across the sand.
Wildly the ocean screams,
Shimmering with the sunbeams.

Magically the ocean dances,
Bubbles on the top prances.
It rolls its eyes at you and me,
The fearless, daring, seething sea.

Eventually, the sea will slumber,
Just as still as a cucumber.
Very calmly the ocean sleeps,
Covering all the creatures it keeps.

In the morning it will awaken,
Feasting on the lives it's taken.
Afterwards it'll stretch and yawn,
Whilst tiny baby fish are born.

Coughing, spluttering and sneezing,
It's caught cold because it is freezing.
Once again it begins to rest,
That's when the sea is at its best!

Holly Webster (10)
Balshaw Lane Primary School, Euxton

The Changing Waterfall

Gushing water pours down
Landing in a splash!

Glistening drops sparkle in the sunlight
Can you see the marvellous glitter?

Lively and bubbly
It's as if the waterfall is alive.

It roars with almighty power over the slippery rocks
Which struggle to survive.

Mist falls down on the waterfall
As it gives it a shower
Staring into its eyes, you see joy and peace!
So do stare, he won't take offence.

He's not like others, he doesn't mind
If you take a ride on him, but you wouldn't dare.

I left my waterfall for a while
When I returned, it wasn't there
This waterfall was different
Frozen icicles dangle down
Oh, I wonder where my waterfall went?

Lydia Brooks (10)
Balshaw Lane Primary School, Euxton

There Is Rhythm All Around

There is rhythm all around
In the sea, the rocks, the air
The crashing waves booming
Against the rocks by the seashore
In fields of beautiful pansies
I spy a bee buzzing angrily
At the flowers bending gracefully

There is rhythm all around
At the beach and the desert
Shells are snapping unexpectedly
As I take my evening walk
In the desert the sand is crunching
As camels tread
The cactus' water wishing
And washing in its inners

There is rhythm all around
Even in the animals
Like sheep prancing around in the burning sun
And tigers growling at their prey
Rhythm.

Sam Moore (9)
Balshaw Lane Primary School, Euxton

The Waterfall

The waterfall is spectacular,
Water gushing down,
Making the current go faster in time.

With the sun dazzling over,
Making the water gleam,
Beautifully!

As you walk along the bank,
Getting closer,
You can see the water vapour splashing the air!

Each drip or gush
Makes the water tumble down
Even faster!

Twirling around,
Escaping, going in different directions,
Stretching like gum!

Roaring, splashing,
Exploding ferociously,
The waterfall starts again.

Jessica Elizabeth Nelson (11)
Balshaw Lane Primary School, Euxton

The Waterfall

Splinters hang out
Of the icy picture.
Icicles twirling around each other
While they effortlessly crash down to the ground
As they melt.

Drop by drop
The spectacular reflections glare at the waterfall.
The more the sun gazes and shines
The more the waterfall cries.

The rocks stick out
And make the waterfall gush out excitedly
As it rushes rapidly
In different directions.

The beautiful waterfall
Smashes against the rocks
Vaporising them.

Daniel Haselden (10)
Balshaw Lane Primary School, Euxton

The Glorious Waterfall

Gushing swiftly, twirling effortlessly
The startling waterfall continued to impress.
It stands out like a tree amongst a field of flowers
Its loud splashing sound makes the vapour sparkle in the sun.
As it continues to flow
The mist that surrounds it makes it hard to see anything.
You can't see the top of the gorgeous waterfall standing so high
Just the pouring sheets of water.
Thrashing down into the deep plunge pool
Within the bubbling, frothy water.

Rachel Tincello (11)
Balshaw Lane Primary School, Euxton

The Waterfall

Like a never-ending rainfall;
The waterfall dived menacingly to the ground.
Splashing and swirling, creeping and crashing;
Water gushed and rushed effortlessly below.
Eating away at the rocks;
Making it more powerful!

Swiftly turning, water raced to the pools below
The long stick-like water thrashed down the rocky face.
The water roars, unbreakable - a closed gate,
Nothing can demolish its reign . . .
A spectacular sight;
Nothing compares to the natural beauty of a waterfall.
Frantically racing to the ground,
To smash the surface!

Thomas Holmes (10)
Balshaw Lane Primary School, Euxton

The Waterfall In Disguise

The sun against the waterfall makes it gleam,
But as peaceful as this may seem,
This is only a disguise,
Just wait until it comes alive . . .

As the wind picks up, the water shakes,
One sudden wave and the water's awake,
Far from happy and scowling inside,
The livid water and rock face collide.

The poor fish that live in this stream,
Never get to fulfil their dream,
You see, this waterfall is so deadly,
It could turn you into a human pie medley.

Ellis Hawkins (11)
Balshaw Lane Primary School, Euxton

The Amazing Waterfall

The waterfall comes gushing and twirling
Over the knobbly rocks.
It booms as it crashes
Against the rocky surface.

Swiftly and effortlessly the water booms
Making little water sprays.
Rushing and gushing
Creating a battle of foam.

Thrilling and spilling
The extraordinary water.
Splashing and spraying,
The waterfall roars and rushes against each other.

Twirling and whirling
The water booms with terror.
Gracefully, the water starts
To calm his temper!

Emelia Rose Carter (10)
Balshaw Lane Primary School, Euxton

Raging Waterfall

Bursting out of the rocks,
Effortlessly pouring,
Crashing down with terror
Like lava from a volcano.

Rapidly banging against the edge
Of the hillside.
Roaring like a dragon
Searching for help.

Continuously splashing,
Like splinters of water.
Shooting down
Into a gushing river.

Gradually pouring,
Down, down, down!
Like a circuit of water,
Never-ending!

Nikkita Kaur Birk (11)
Balshaw Lane Primary School, Euxton

The Waterfall

Splinters of ice cling to your face,
Like a monstrous magnet.
The icy water erodes the rocks,
With a giant boom and shatter.
No life exists within the icy tomb,
What could be in there?

The waterfall looks so strange,
Frozen on its way down,
Looking like an icy window.
Only the slightest of water is still alive,
Trickling like a stream.

Even though it is a perishing day,
The sun still shines down,
Making it melt swiftly.
Twirling and whirling,
Gushing and whooshing.
The waterfall continues . . .
It's like being in a dream.

Charlotte Walsh (10)
Balshaw Lane Primary School, Euxton

Remembrance Poem

A never-ending sea of red,
Could you be next to fall down, dead?
As you continue to stand so proud,
Your friends decay beneath the clouds.

All are injured and distressed,
The battlefield is now a mess,
Littered with bodies and uniforms,
All the more for us to mourn.

Your death was thanks to insanity,
If only there was such a thing as immortality,
Our thoughts are sad and melancholy,
Now you're gone, we're oh so sorry.

Every day, approaching death,
Who knows which second holds their last breath?
Yet, what gives them the hope? What gives them the power?
. . . A very special crimson flower.

Charlotte Bradbury (11)
Balshaw Lane Primary School, Euxton

The Waterfall

The waterfall is swirling and twirling
Over the rocks.

It booms as it crashes
Against the rocky wall.

Rushing and gushing, creating a bath of foam
It clashes with the rocks.

It's so thrilling
When it's spilling all over the place!

Whirling everywhere
The two waves rush towards each other.

Gracefully, the water starts to calm his temper
And then there is only a drip-drop left.

Kirsty Pope (10)
Balshaw Lane Primary School, Euxton

The Misty Waterfall!

The misty waterfall,
Spectacularly splashing
Against the rock pool.
The sound of water crackles
As it rushes,
Splashing between the rocks
At the bottom, twirling amazingly.
Water stretching
Like chewing gum
Frothing furiously.
Bubbling like a Jacuzzi
Into the plunge pool,
Stunning, throwing its power
Down towards the rocks!

Brandon Moseley (10)
Balshaw Lane Primary School, Euxton

The Taken Ocean

The ocean peacefully lapped against the shore,
Dancing happily, retreating onto the shingle stones.

The ocean sometimes can be cruel and destructive,
Destroying fish schools, running them down with each different wave.

It is home to many, some smaller than a penny,
Dolphins and sharks fight for their place, finding food in extraordinary ways.

Ships that sink cause oil leaks,
That even the kings of the sea cannot even stop.

They kill the fish and eat what they have taken
From the powerful lair of the ocean.

Harvey Unsworth (11)
Balshaw Lane Primary School, Euxton

Anything

Monkeys with a glimpse of an eye
Weeping streams that cry
A bin lid that clangs and crashes
A glass cup that bangs and smashes
A volcano that speaks smoke
A roaring stripy tiger that has just woke
A bird that sings and squeals
A fish . . . I think it's an eel
A giraffe and a long-necked duck
A little pink pig that rolls in the muck
A fox has caught a bird
An idea has just occurred . . . !

Melissa McGhee (9)
Balshaw Lane Primary School, Euxton

The Ocean Blue

Flaming up, joining sides with the sun,
The ocean screamed as if shot by a gun.

Crushing waves smashed against the glistening rocks,
Making the sea weep along with the birds in flocks.

Spitting turtles and crabs onto the shiny seabed,
The ocean bubbled sucking them back instead.

As the moon rises up and the tide rides in,
Springing aquatic fish sailing through with their fin.

Alas, the sun has gone down and the moon stays bright,
The ocean stays happy, whispering, 'Goodnight . . .'

Joshua Bergin (11)
Balshaw Lane Primary School, Euxton

The Night Sky Above Us!

Clouds
Fly across
The sky, the
Stars shine silver
Sparkling and twinkling,
The black night sky like a woollen
Blanket, has a big button glowing with
Joy, light fills the black sky with
Happiness and joy, as day
Appears the stars and
The moon say goodbye
Waiting for the next
Calm night to
Awake
Them!

Ebony Taylor (10)
Bentley High Street Primary School, Bentley

I Will Put In My Box . . .

(Based on 'Magic Box' by Kit Wright)

I will put in my box . . .
The smiles of happy children
The sweet smell of a groomed horse
A strand of the finest silk.

I will put in my box . . .
The voice of all languages
A baby's first laugh
The sound of a horse's gallop.

I will design my box . . .
On the lid there is the softest snow
In the edges is a cold shape of a young pony's hoof
All around there is the scent of the hay, strong chaff.

I will take my box . . .
I will take my box everywhere I shall go
Even on scary roller coasters
My box will be thrown into the blue sky, high as can be
And will come down in the future
And land in my baby child's arms.

Julieanne Wootton (11)
Bentley High Street Primary School, Bentley

Hot Days

H eatwaves run through the Earth
O ut at sea trying to surf
T ired so you try and relax

D ark red sunburn on people's backs
A lways beware of sunstroke
Y oung children likely to choke
S weat drops from your head whilst you are bright red.

Jordan Hendry (11)
Bentley High Street Primary School, Bentley

One To Another

Circle
To a rectangle
Rectangle to a triangle
And a triangle to a
Square.

Trees
Chopped down
Turned into paper
Paper is written on
And turned into
Books.

Smooth
Water from the lake
Sails down to the waterfall
And when it arrives, it gets faster
And when the water is at the bottom, it is
Rough.

Cats
Are cute and cuddly
At day
But in the night
They are fierce
Animals.

White
Walls as they begin
But near the end
The white walls change to
Black.

Blue
Skies cover the shaking earth
At day, but in the night
Skies change to
Black.

Michael Glassner Leadenham (10)
Bentley High Street Primary School, Bentley

Rooney

R ooney, the star of the show
O ver the top and in the net
O n the yellow and now the red
N o more goals, out for the season
E very move he makes, it's always a good one
Y es, he's done it, saved England from a draw

S trikers always get the goals
T he master of the forwards
R ooney never stops running
I n striking, he is the main man
K ing of Man U, top man of England
E ven maybe the top of the world
R ubbish teams never win, especially when Rooney's in.

Lewis Gilbert (10)
Bentley High Street Primary School, Bentley

Summer Days

S un shines for days to come
U mbrellas are not needed
M arvellous water sparkles in the sun
M ore hot days for everyone
E njoyable things for you to do
R eally enjoying summertime, in the summer the sun will shine.

Bethany Copestake (11)
Bentley High Street Primary School, Bentley

Guess What?

The opposite of the living,
Only one thing on its mind.

Cities are its hunting grounds,
Any living thing is satisfying.

Eyes a-glowing red,
Body covered in blood of others.

Suspicious limbs missing,
Human shape.

Scary as a vampire,
Razor-sharp teeth

A zombie!

Kyle Cordon (10)
Bentley High Street Primary School, Bentley

What Am I?

I am big, I am brown, also green
I smell like nothing at all
I taste rather horrible, you would never like to try me
I feel soft and rough, but sometimes wrinkly
I remind you of the breeze
I am leaves and trees.

I am blue, I am wavy
I smell like nothing
I taste salty
I feel very watery
I remind you of the sky
I am the waves.

Jasmine Lailey (9)
Bentley High Street Primary School, Bentley

World War Two

W ars fighting for the world
O pen fire at Germans
R ampaging with their massive tanks
L orries full of weapons
D estroying buildings madly

W eapons going insanely mad
A ir Force coming to bomb countries
R ampaging from town to town

T anks blowing half of the country up
W acky people getting shot
O h, it went on and on till the Germans gave up.

Lochlan Cunningham (8)
Bentley High Street Primary School, Bentley

Kris' Acrostic

K ind as a teacher
R eads books
I ce cream mad
S uper Pickard

P recious as a rose
I s so annoying
C ool Kris
K icking all the footballs
A lways making trouble
R uns fast
D odges people.

Kris Pickard (11)
Bentley High Street Primary School, Bentley

Dragons

D ragons' scales are as hard as a stone, so they can protect it when it is fighting
R apidly a dragon pounded into the air and fled from the battle
A s the dragon was being clawed by its enemy, its powerful horns tried to protect it
G ruesome dragons rip up their prey and eat its guts and body
O n a dragon's back it has flames that make your hair turn into ash
N asty dragons breathe fire, scalding and hair blowing at humans to make them petrified
S upreme dragons make powerful tornados with their cotton-like wings.

Liam Pidcock (10)
Bentley High Street Primary School, Bentley

My Kitten

Door scratcher
Hand licker
Carpet clawer
Loud purrer
Champion cuddler
Fierce growler
Curious explorer
Cute sleeper
Fast runner
Daring jumper
My kitten, Misty!

Jennifer Field (11)
Bentley High Street Primary School, Bentley

What Am I?

I am black and I have a wet nose
I have long legs and sharp toes
I smell like a rat and I'm always sat
I taste like a piece of meat and I love to sleep
I hear rats and they always scratch
And I hear other things, like cats
But they tend not to scratch
I feel like a bunch of feathers
And I love to jump about in them
And I remind you of a snugly-bugly teddy
What am I?

Olivia Olsen (9)
Bentley High Street Primary School, Bentley

What Am I?

I look like a big shaped blob
I taste like a beautiful pudding
I remind you of birthdays and celebrations
I feel nice and soft
I look like something you can't resist
I taste like a delightful, filling pudding
I remind you of good times
I smell of cream
I feel like a sponge
What am I?
A cake!

Rebecca Vickers (9)
Bentley High Street Primary School, Bentley

My Mum's Bump

M y mum's bump is big
Y ep, big, big, big

M um's bump is going to explode
U ntil bump goes
M y mum is going to be lazy
S ister won't be like that Mum says

B ump is going to be out soon
U ntil stress starts, I think I need to have a lie down
M ummy needs her sleep too
P op! Bump is finally out!

Bethany Baugh (10)
Bentley High Street Primary School, Bentley

What Am I?

I'm blue and new
I smell of pens and lead
I taste yucky, like a ducky
I feel old, but I'm not
I remind you of small.

I hold pencils in
I hold lead in bed
I sometimes hold paperclips in
What do you think I am?
I am a blue pencil pot!

Jack Livingstone (9)
Bentley High Street Primary School, Bentley

Burnt Bread

There was an old, wrinkly man,
Who was in his big, fancy house,
He baked some delicious brown bread,
Then he went to his comfy bed.

He woke up smelling the fresh bread,
With his wet mouth watering,
Two hours later, when he woke up . . .
His beautiful bread was burnt!
So he learnt never to fall asleep
Whilst baking bread again!

Chloe Horsfield (10)
Bentley High Street Primary School, Bentley

What Am I?

I look brown and sticky
I smell rather tasty
I feel lumpy and bumpy
I taste like a delight
What am I?

I look like square pieces
I taste like a feast
I smell rather delicious
I feel smooth
I am chocolate!

Chloe Powell (9)
Bentley High Street Primary School, Bentley

Halloween

H alloween is fun at night
A ll go as witches
L oving Halloween tonight
L oving all the treats I get
O h, a ghost is behind me!
W hee! I'm having fun!
E at all the spooky treats I get
E at it! Eat it!
N o more for my tummy.

Sophie Jane Coy (8)
Bentley High Street Primary School, Bentley

All About Nicolette

N ice Nicolette is now 11
I have seven pets
C reative at home
O bviously my baby brother is cute, Jarvis
L ovely blonde hair I have
E at pizza
T omatoes are horrible
T alkative Nicolette chatter, chatter and chatter
E njoying the sun all the time, well that's all about me!

Nicolette Marsh (11)
Bentley High Street Primary School, Bentley

What Am I?

I look so sweet
I smell of wheat
I taste of mint
I see so far
I fly so fast
I hear like a broadcast
I remind you of the colour gold
What am I?
A golden eagle!

Luke Jackson (8)
Bentley High Street Primary School, Bentley

What Am I?

I'm big and slow, like a rhino
I carry a lot of weight, like my mate
I feel like slime
I smell of sludge
I taste like mud
I look brown like sludge
When I'm nice, I taste like a fish on a dish
What am I?
I'm a slug!

Liam Macey (9)
Bentley High Street Primary School, Bentley

Mrs Throssell!

She is lovely
She is sweet
She does not shout
She is fun
She is happy
She is the most friendly person
She is the best teacher ever
She is a bunch of sweet roses
She is Mrs Throssell!

Charlie Leek (11)
Bentley High Street Primary School, Bentley

My Friend, Mason

He is as amazing as an acrobat
He is as helpful as a doctor
He is as funny as a clown
He is as ginger as an orange
He is as exciting as a fairground
He is as playful as a ball
He is as healthy as a fruit
He is as skinny as a stick
He is my best friend, Mason.

Josh Maddison (11)
Bentley High Street Primary School, Bentley

Chocolate!

C hocolate is like living in Heaven
H ollow, filled, they are the types for me
O h, so sensational
C an be used to make sculptures of any kind
O bviously I love chocolate
L ife revolves around dreamy chocolate
A ero, Galaxy, Cadbury's, which one shall I choose?
T he sensation tingles my tastebuds
E ver so creamy!

Megan Louise Todd (11)
Bentley High Street Primary School, Bentley

Horses

Horses are the best
Better than all the rest
Brilliant at racing they are
But they can't drive a car!

Although my horse can't stand loud sounds
She is as fast as a hound
Foals are very cute, but . . .
They would never try the *flute!*

Coralena Ann Dear (10)
Bentley High Street Primary School, Bentley

Rugby

R ugby is a fun and active sport
U s children love rugby
G rowing up means you get much better
B eats basketball, football and tennis
Y ou'd think everything beats it, but you're wrong.

Elliot Sprakes (8)
Bentley High Street Primary School, Bentley

My Mum

She is as pink as a carnation
She is as bright as teachers in school
She is as busy as London
She is as warm as a summer's day
She is as fun as a fair
She is as sparkly as the biggest night star
She is as beautiful as a red rose
She is my mum.

Mason Owen (11)
Bentley High Street Primary School, Bentley

All About Courtney

C reative Courtney is 11
O bviously she loves hanging with her mates
U pside down like a monkey
R unning hastily, she always falls over
T alkative Courtney loves to chat
N oisy as a bulldozer
E xcellent at gymnastics
Y ummy as a gummy bear.

Courtney Shaw (11)
Bentley High Street Primary School, Bentley

Rabbit

R abbits are cute, fluffy and soft
A lways got a little nose
B ut when it comes to stroking, they might just take your nose
B uddies, they are nice and friendly
I like rabbits, as long as they don't fight me
T imes they are scruffy.

Charlotte Parkes (8)
Bentley High Street Primary School, Bentley

What Am I?

I look like a furry animal
I smell like shampoo
I sound like a rabbit
I am soft, like a dog
I feel like a kitten
I remind you of the jungle
What am I?
A monkey!

Liam Wortley (9)
Bentley High Street Primary School, Bentley

What Am I?

I am big and golden
I smell like soap and water
I feel soft, like fluff
I sound like *woof, woof, woof*
I taste like nothing at all
I remind you of a house pet
What am I?
A golden retriever!

Spiderlouise Williams (8)
Bentley High Street Primary School, Bentley

What Am I?

I look sticky and brown sometimes
I smell rather delicious
I taste all melty
I feel lumpy and bumpy
What am I?
I am chocolate!

Kirra Nimmo (9)
Bentley High Street Primary School, Bentley

Football

F antastic goals
O riginal skills
O blong-shaped pitches
T all goalposts
B est pitches
A wesome games
L arge pitches
L ong-lasting matches.

Joe Benson (11)
Bentley High Street Primary School, Bentley

Colours

C olours are bright
O range is a colour
L ovely colours, they're so bright
O range, orange, what a lovely colour
U is a letter, but that's not a colour
R ed is like fire
S o that's the end.

McKenzie Baker-Ward (8)
Bentley High Street Primary School, Bentley

England

E ngland are the best
N ever have they lost
G roups of team passing
L ong games watched nervously
A ngry people as well
N o! Don't let them win
D ad cheers really loud.

Michael Robert Cooper (8)
Bentley High Street Primary School, Bentley

What Am I?

I look like a bat
I smell like a rat
I taste like a mat
I feel like a cat
I see a lot of light
What am I?
I am a bird.

Morgan Newton (9)
Bentley High Street Primary School, Bentley

Ocean

O ctopuses swim in the water
C reatures lurk all around
E verywhere I look there's water
A shark's bite could chop off a head
N ever go too close to a shark, because you'll lose your head!

Samuel Bowker (8)
Bentley High Street Primary School, Bentley

Football Crazy

The game is so great
Commentated by Ryan Tate
Ronaldo kicked something into the sky
Yeah man, so high
Oh, no! It's too late!

Marlie Rodney (10)
Bentley High Street Primary School, Bentley

Sad Day

The day I went to funky town,
The mayor was wearing his shiny crown,
But then I sat down,
With a big frown,
Because he gave it to Gordon Brown!

Joshua James Vidler (10)
Bentley High Street Primary School, Bentley

My Black Cat

I once had a cat
Which was black
She screeched and scratched
At other cats
And then she met her purrfect match!

Harrison Stephens (10)
Bentley High Street Primary School, Bentley

What Am I?

I am purple, round and fat
I smell like mud and taste of blood
I am sloppy, like a slug
Because I lie in the mud
I'm a hippopotamus!

Chloe Jade Read (8)
Bentley High Street Primary School, Bentley

Diverse World

You can't really hide it,
It will always be there,
Because in the outside world,
It's not really fair.

We look outside our window
And see a road full of cars,
They look outside their slums
And see rubbish heaps and gang wars.

We complain about the weather,
Or if our mum won't buy us that new phone,
But they walk four miles or more,
Just to get to a filthy water hose.

Next time you have got a cough
And are staying off school,
Think of them who are fighting for their lives,
With diseases that can't be cured.

The world is diverse
And full of extremes,
Some children have everything,
Whilst others only have dreams.

Olivia Cawthorn (11)
Birdwell Primary School, Birdwell

Pets

Pets, pets
There are all kinds
Fat ones, thin ones
Small ones, big ones
I love pets!

Mia Taylor (8)
Fulwood & Cadley CP School, Fulwood

Little Red Riding Hood!

Little Red Riding Hood went to the woods one day,
To deliver some flowers to her grandma.

On the way there she met the big bad wolf,
Who tried to take them from her.

She ran away from the wolf to her grandma's house
And tiptoed round to the back door.

She opened it slowly and locked it with the key,
But was amazed at what she saw.

There was the wolf in her grandma's clothes,
Inside her grandma's bed.

Where is my grandma? She quietly thought,
But Little Red Riding Hood said:

'What big ears you have Grandma,
I've not noticed them before.'

'All the better to hear you with, my dear,' said the wolf
And let out a gentle snore.

'What big eyes you have, Grandma,
I've not noticed them before.'

'All the better to see you with, my dear,' said the wolf
And let out a gentle roar.

'What big teeth you have, Grandma,
I've not noticed them before.'

'All the better to eat you with, my dear!' snapped the wolf
And opened his big wide jaw.

She ran out of the house, screaming, 'Wolf!'
As its jaws were snapping behind.

A woodsman appeared with a big, strong axe
And caught it just in time.

The wolf spat out her frail little grandma,
Who was looking a little worse for wear.

'Grandma, I'm so happy to see you,' said Little Red Riding Hood,
'You gave me quite a scare!'

The woodsman took the wolf to the forest, far, far away
And was never to be seen again.

Little Red Riding Hood and her grandma went home
And I'm happy to say, *the end!*

Laura Jackson (10)
Fulwood & Cadley CP School, Fulwood

Guess Who?

Goal scorer
Team player
Pass master
Strong tackler
Goal stopper
Corner taker
Position keeper
Long thrower
Fair player
Tactical maker
Feisty defender
Brainy midfielder
Striking striker
Fast thinker
Physically stronger
Positive thinker
Great listener
Crowd persuader
Good encourager
100% giver
Determined learner
Fans adorer
A footballer!

Dilan Vadher (11)
Fulwood & Cadley CP School, Fulwood

A Wolf And Three Pigs

Once upon a starry night
There was such a dreadful sight
A mother telling her sons to find new places
This made the boys pull all kinds of faces
One house was made out of straw
He hoped it wouldn't collapse to the floor
Another house was made out of sticks
And inside there was a poster of the New York Knicks
The final house was made out of bricks
It was much stronger than the house of sticks
Now a big bad wolf was in the trees
He was also itching with all his fleas
The big bad wolf thought of an idea
And it would make the pigs dance with fear
The big bad wolf went to the straw house
He was as quiet as a mouse
When the wolf asked to come in
The pig said, 'Not by the hairs on my chinny-chin-chin!'
The wolf got mad and blew the house down
This made the pig moan and frown
The wolf followed the first pig to the stick house
This time the wolf was much louder than a mouse
They still wouldn't let the wolf come in
Then through the letterbox poked the wolf with a pin
The wolf got mad
And away went the stick pad
They ran down to their brother's house
And they still wouldn't let the wolf join them
The wolf tried to blow the house down
But it stood still and the wolf started to frown
The wolf wanted to come down the chimney
But the pigs made a plan
They boiled some water and put it in a pan

When the wolf came down
He burnt his bum and ran off
The wolf was never seen again
And they all lived happily ever after!

James Nicolas Bracken (10)
Fulwood & Cadley CP School, Fulwood

Guess Who?

He's fearless
Barcelona player
World's best striker

Ecstatic runner
Skilful dribbler

Determined worker
Strong tackler

Argentinean
Goal minion

He's 22
Above all of you

World Cup hero
Better than Cristiano Ronaldo!

He's a trophy holder
Title holder

Who is he?
Lionel Messi!

Vishal Gohil (11)
Fulwood & Cadley CP School, Fulwood

Guess Who?

Goal scorer,
Goal maker,
Team captain,
Goal passer,
Game attacker,
Game packer,
Hates losing,
Loves winning,
Goal hopper,
Goal stopper,
Top goal scorer,
Hungry for trophies,
He might be joining Barca
But he says bye-bye Barca
Cesc Fabregas.

Jay Bond (11)
Fulwood & Cadley CP School, Fulwood

It's Good To Be Me!

Maybe I don't smoke,
Maybe I don't sing,
Maybe I don't dance like you,
But hey, that's just who I am!

Maybe my trainers are tatty,
Maybe my clothes are old,
Maybe I don't wear make-up,
But hey, that's just who I am!

Maybe you tease,
Maybe you bully,
So just show some respect for who I am . . .
Coz *it's good to be me!*

Lydia Dixon
Fulwood & Cadley CP School, Fulwood

Holidays

On my holiday,
I went to Norway,
It's very cold,
But I was told,
To wear a jacket,
But all I was doing was trying to pop my crisp packet,
I saw a beautiful landscape,
But it was a very peculiar shape,
I saw an ape in the sea,
He was called Lee,
I have to say,
It was a long day.

Hassan Bakhat (8)
Fulwood & Cadley CP School, Fulwood

Elephants

Elephants, elephants, big and strong
Live in India and have a trunk that's very long
Long ears that flap, flap, flap
And tusks that are ivory-white
Skin that's wrinkly and grey
I don't think they eat hay
Wanted by hunters for their valuable tusks
Be careful elephants, who you trust
Useful are elephants for their strength
Can move large logs and not be out of breath
Elephant, elephant, as big as a house
How come you're scared of a little mouse?

Khalil Patel (8)
Fulwood & Cadley CP School, Fulwood

My Hamsters

M ichael Jackson
Y akult is his gorgeous twin brother, but I've got plenty more
   hamsters, I can't name them all

H e runs around his cage like a mad chicken (Yakult)
A fter a few years, unfortunately they will die!
M e and my hamsters would be best buddies if they were human
S leeping in my hand - they are *soooo* cute
T rying to lay them down in their soft beds without waking them up
E veryone when they come round always says, 'Aww!'
R ascals they are, but cute
S weet, loveable hamsters!

Megan Haigh (10)
Fulwood & Cadley CP School, Fulwood

The Majestic Tiger!

As beautiful as the morning light,
Raging with power and might,
You never know when it might bite.
The best hunter at any time,
Blends with the grass as green as lime,
Hunts in the forest of pine.
Always feared but also hunted,
Every day kicked and punted,
But never ever disrespected.
They shall never lose the extinction fight,
The breeding grip still very tight.

Katharine Beavers (11)
Fulwood & Cadley CP School, Fulwood

The Season Song

S ummer blaze
E ccentric rays
A mazing heat
S uncream cheat
O minous wind
N ever silent

S pring lingers
O ne touch fingers
N ature grows
G ushing waterfall.

Conor Lambert (11)
Fulwood & Cadley CP School, Fulwood

Summer

S ummertime is when you enjoy the gorgeous weather, play out late and eat lots of ice cream
U nder the sun, children have fun and enjoy barbecues with their families
M orning sun is shining and another day of excitement is arriving
M others are relaxing on the beach and children are swimming joyfully
E veryone is going on holiday and people are playing and enjoying themselves
R oses are blooming with beautiful petals and vibrant colours.

Arooj Ali (9)
Fulwood & Cadley CP School, Fulwood

Pollution

Our planet is dying and we are killing it,
Smoke, fire and ash alike,
They are destroying our trees
And our planet,
We need to save it now
And stop cutting down trees,
If Earth dies and crashes out of orbit,
We will die with it and so will every creature on Earth,
We are killing Mother Nature and she will want revenge,
So everybody, stop pollution, before it's too late and everything ends.

Adam Suleman (10)
Fulwood & Cadley CP School, Fulwood

The Qualities Of Football

F ast and energetic it gets your heart pumping
O verlooking your team, hoping for the best
O pponents can be either really easy or as hard as a brick
T actics, man-marking, positional awareness, zonal positioning
   are vital if you want to succeed
B ut without losers there are no winners
A ll the star players live their lives for the beautiful game
L ots of passionate supporters, all very optimistic
L ooking at your team's star player, you dream of him scoring.

Joe Hyde (11)
Fulwood & Cadley CP School, Fulwood

Deserted Deserts

D eserted, vast landscape, glowing in the blistering sun!
E lephants randomly stomping in the bright, yellow sand!
S andstorms sweeping across the wide land while the small
   animals burrow for shelter
E choing noises of the domestic animals calling to their family
R epeatedly, the vultures aggressively rip the meat off
   the rotting lion!
T actically, the cunning scorpion approaches its unaware prey
S corching hot weather quickly heats up the cold-blooded reptiles.

Christopher Dewhurst (11)
Fulwood & Cadley CP School, Fulwood

My Hamster

Charley is my cool hamster
She is as fast as a tiger
But smaller than a mouse

She likes to do the monkey bars
And she climbs into jars
But she loves sleeping and eating

Charley loves her playtime
Her favourite part is playing in her ball!

Poppy Wigg (11)
Fulwood & Cadley CP School, Fulwood

The Ocean's Lullaby

Every night the ocean calls,
He sings to me his special song,
Calling out across the waves,
His lullaby surrounds me.

The moonlight shines across the sea,
She dances across the waves,
If I ever wake up and it's all just a dream,
I'll always remember . . . the ocean's lullaby.

Calista Gibirdi (10)
Fulwood & Cadley CP School, Fulwood

The Car That Took The World By Surprise!

B eautiful noise as you turn the key and start the engine
U nbelievable speed
G racious and air-resistant
A merican muscle, strong and trustworthy
T remendous interiors (leather seats)
T remendous style and convertible roof
I nternational best-seller and one of the most-loved cars!

Adam Stuart Wilkinson (11)
Fulwood & Cadley CP School, Fulwood

Daffodil

D affodils dangle in the rain
A ll the flowers have an orange trumpet
F ields of beautiful spring happiness
F ull of blooms in the park
O ur yellow sheets herald the day
D elicious lemons remind me of spring
I love March, April and May
L ittle bunches of flowers.

Yasser Karim Khan (8)
Fulwood & Cadley CP School, Fulwood

Dad

When I was one he held me tight
When I was two he gave me a bath
When I was three he read me a story
When I was four he took me to school
When I was five he called me Princess
When I was six he tickled me
When I was seven he came to watch my ballet show
Now I am eight I say I love him.

Lorna Clitheroe (8)
Fulwood & Cadley CP School, Fulwood

My Mum

Tan lover
Good mother
Hates Big Brother
Cake baker
Sleep faker
Slow waker
Oven hater
Patient waiter.

Jade Preston (10)
Fulwood & Cadley CP School, Fulwood

The Evil Land

Spiky music here and there,
Spaceships landing everywhere,
Robots taking over the land,
Shooting lasers in each hand,
It's dull, scary, dark and bad,
It's dreadful, hot, vicious and sad,
It's crazy, dangerous, mad and more,
There's fire dotted on the floor,
Devils, scary faces and graves,
Moaning, spaceships, masks and slaves,
A voodoo doll is a terrible thing,
They can even kill the king
And when you come to visit this place,
You might want to pick up your pace,
So you don't get caught by these evil things,
But if I were you, don't come for anything!

Emily Garner (10)
Linton-on-Ouse Primary School, Linton-on-Ouse

The Northern Counties

I'm Envious

I'm envious,
Everyone on my table has got one,
They boast and tease,
I sit here waiting, waiting for hometime,
To ask my mum again and again,
But every time the answer's, 'No!'
My heart shrivels; my eyes fill with tears,
I become more and more bored.

If I had one,
I could take it for walks, play fetch,
All sorts of things,
I'm envious; it's not fair,
It's every day and it's not nice.

I would like a dog.

Jessica Luck (11)
Linton-on-Ouse Primary School, Linton-on-Ouse

My Dog

I love my dog,
My dog loves me,
We walk together
And play together,
As fun as fun can be.

But . . .

I still love my dog
And my dog still loves me,
But he is no longer with me,
So we can't walk together
And we can't play together,
As fun as fun can be.

Miles Manfield (11)
Linton-on-Ouse Primary School, Linton-on-Ouse

Red

Red is angry,
Red is sad.
Red is scary,
Red is bad.
Red is bloodstains on soldiers of war,
Red is the poster on the back of your door.

Red is your friends in the grave,
Red is the colour of a slave.
Red is the picture on a bottle of pop,
Red is the sign that says   *stop!*

Next time you see the colour of red,
Make sure you've listened to what I've said!

Robert Garner (10)
Linton-on-Ouse Primary School, Linton-on-Ouse

Aliens In Action

I can hear them coming . . . *aliens!*
Coming to bring destruction to the Earth
And turn us into dust
We are doomed!
We won't stand a chance against them!
Their UFOs will take us to their home world
And make us work for all our lives
Their fleet will soon come to destroy the leftovers of us
The mothership will land and unload their builders
And make breeding pits
They will build a new race of . . . *aliens!*

Conor Aston (10)
Linton-on-Ouse Primary School, Linton-on-Ouse

A Recipe For Disaster

Take one stressed mum with crying baby,
Nagging toddler and wonky buggy.
Mix with some smoking teenagers, with leaking bus shelter,
Sprinkle a rainstorm on top, with a rattling bus.
Mixed with a busy supermarket with old grannies,
Then bake for 40-45 minutes
And that's a recipe for disaster!

Amelia Brown (10)
Linton-on-Ouse Primary School, Linton-on-Ouse

My Fear

That day will never be forgotten,
Emotions that day were all mixed-up.
I couldn't speak - all that came out was tears,
I couldn't move - the shock was too big.

One word - eleven letters

Afghanistan.

Bethany McClelland (11)
Linton-on-Ouse Primary School, Linton-on-Ouse

A Trip To McDonald's

Take one restaurant in a busy town,
Add lots of hungry children,
Pour over some ice-cold drinks,
Cover with hot burgers with a slice of cheese,
Soak in the delicious smell,
Shower with pickles on top.

Harry Mannion (9)
Linton-on-Ouse Primary School, Linton-on-Ouse

Joy

What does it smell like?
Joy smells like the beautiful spring, the smell of the magnifying flowers.
What does it remind you of?
Joy reminds you of a joyful moment in your life, the days you have fun and the days that you are happy.
What does it taste like?
Joy tastes like anything, roast pork, hot dogs and even cheese and crackers.
What colour is it?
Joy is any colour you want it to be, yellow, green, they are happy colours.
Where can you find it?
You can find joy in your heart, children, fun and laughter.
What does it sound like?
Joy sounds like laughter and many more fun things.
What does it look like?
Joy looks like children playing, laughing and enjoying themselves.

John Bonsall (10)
Out Rawcliffe CE School, Out Rawcliffe

Happiness

What does it look like?
Little children smiling and laughing in the blazing sun.
What does it taste like?
It tastes like a four cheese pizza with salami and a crust filled with cheese.
What colour is it?
The colour of happiness is yellow, because the sun shines on the children playing football.
Where can you find it?
The best place where you can find happiness, is deep in the depths of your heart.
What does it sound like?
Happiness sounds like laughter and happy sounds.
What does it smell like?
Happiness is a beautiful smell and it fills your nostrils with a brilliant scent.
What does it remind you of?
It reminds me of going on holiday and splashing in the pool.

John Robert Davies (11)
Out Rawcliffe CE School, Out Rawcliffe

Love

What colour is it?
Red, pink and white, because pink is the lips, red for the heart and white is for the wedding dress.
Where can you find it?
You can find love in your heart.
What does it remind you of?
Your happy times in the past.
What does it sound like?
Love sounds like it is romantic.
What does it smell of?
Love smells of roses.
What does it taste like?
Love tastes like lipstick.
What does it look like?
It looks like love.

Kimberley Jane Newhouse (9)
Out Rawcliffe CE School, Out Rawcliffe

Laughter

What does it remind me of?
It reminds me of when something delightful happens
And when people are enthusiastic.
What does it look like?
It looks like people's eyes watering and cheerfulness.
What does it sound like?
It sounds like so much fun.
Where can you find it?
Inside your heart.
What colour is it?
It is white, because it's just a sound.
What does it smell like?
It smells like fish on a plate.
What does it taste like?
It tastes like burnt sausage!

Anna Jenkinson (9)
Out Rawcliffe CE School, Out Rawcliffe

Sadness

Where can you find it?
You find it in your heart.
What does it remind you of?
It reminds you of a funeral.
What colour is it?
Black, because it is dark.
What does it look like?
It looks like drops of tears.
What does it taste like?
It tastes like teardrops.
What does it smell like?
It smells like sad people.
What does it sound like?
It sounds like loads of people crying.

James Guthrie (10)
Out Rawcliffe CE School, Out Rawcliffe

Laughter

What colour is it?
Laughter is purple.
What does it smell of?
Laughter smells nice.
Where can you find it?
Laughter is everywhere.
What does it taste like?
Laughter tastes of toast and honey.
What does it remind you of?
Laughter reminds you of good times.
What does it look like?
Laughter looks happy.
What does it sound like?
Laughter sounds like fun.

Eve MacMillan (8)
Out Rawcliffe CE School, Out Rawcliffe

Silence

What does it taste like?
It tastes like dryness, because you're not saying anything, so your mouth goes dry.
What does it look like?
Nothing.
What does it smell of?
Nothing.
What does it sound like?
It doesn't sound of anything.
Where do you find it?
You can find it anywhere.
What colour is it?
It's transparent.
What does it remind you of?
A dull place.

William Lewis (10)
Out Rawcliffe CE School, Out Rawcliffe

Joy

What does joy sound like?
Joy sounds like happiness and clapping.
What does it remind you of?
Joy reminds you of the good times.
Where can you find it?
You can find joy in your heart when you are feeling happy.
What does it taste like?
Joy tastes like the joyous sun that beams down on the world.
What does it look like?
Joy looks like happy faces.
What colour is it?
Joy is glowing yellow, like the sun.
What does it smell of?
Joy smells of happiness.

Anna Charles (9)
Out Rawcliffe CE School, Out Rawcliffe

Sadness

What does it sound like?
A crying child trying to stay alive.
Where can you find it?
It is found underground and all around.
What colour is it?
The colour of darkness and emptiness.
What does it taste of?
It tastes like badness, meanness and the taste of a broken heart.
What does it look like?
The darkness of a deep dungeon.
What does it smell of?
The crying of an abandoned child.
What does it remind you of?
It reminds me of a child forced into labour.

Joshua Philip Kelsall (9)
Out Rawcliffe CE School, Out Rawcliffe

Love

What colour is it?
Love is red, because it is like the sun.
What does it smell like?
Love smells like Chinese.
Where can you find it?
Love is giving your mum a kiss.
What does it taste like?
Love tastes like chocolate.
What does it remind you of?
Love reminds me of my mum.
What does it look like?
Love looks like a heart.
What does it sound like?
Love sounds like an owl.

Alex Wallace (8)
Out Rawcliffe CE School, Out Rawcliffe

The Lion

As he crawls through the long green grass
Paw marks in the mud, leading to the forest
He leaps for his prey
The helpless creature has no escape

As he cries with sad laughter
Whack! He kills the animal
The poor creature's family mourn him
And sadly stride away

The deadly weapon leaps far into the forest
His teeth shining like the sun
Flexible body stretches like rubber
He happily trots away.

Harri Kildear
St Francis of Assisi Catholic Primary School, Skelmersdale

My New Friend . . .

Where am I?
What am I doing?
The bellowing house intrigued me deeply,
By its loud, howling voice,
Its inviting, embracing arms,
I am definitely done for.

As I coolly saunter towards
The strangely loquacious staircase,
He tells me he'll kill me if I get too close,
I'm super scared stiff!

The eerie, screeching banisters have scary,
Sinister snakes,
Like lethal, strangling ropes tightly tied,
Around some unfortunate,
Innocent soul's neck,
Entwined around its wooden body.

My slowly sweating heart skips a beat.

Creak!

A dangling doorway suddenly opens above my little head,
I barely look up;
I am terrified!

A cackling witch in a black pointed hat,
Stares down back at me, with her burning burgundy eyes,
Her rotting teeth shine in the mouldy moonlight
And her brown, hairy warts
Make me cringe.

She picks up a snake, which is hissing with sad laughter
And pets it gently, taking great care,
It is wounded,
The spooky witch waves her impressive magic wand
And *poof!*
The huge cut on the scary snake has completely disappeared.

She gives me the screaming animal,
I hold it with great fear,
It spits at me and green, slimy gunk cloaks my face,
Now I am enveloped in darkness, in a haunted house,
The fact is . . .
I am haunting it!
Where am I?
What am I doing?

Lauren May Shields (11)
St Francis of Assisi Catholic Primary School, Skelmersdale

The Beach

Boom! Crash!
Stella awakens on the bright, golden beach,
As she stares into the light blue sky,
All she can remember is the shiny, newly-painted blue boat
Sinking in the deep blue sea,
As she rises to her feet, soft sand crawls into her toes,
Waves crash angrily against the sandy bay,
Birds sing their morning song,
Like a trumpet puffing its power into the sky,
Trees sway like a plane in the dark night sky,
Hard stones dug into the light sand,
Fewer boats in the dark sea than in the day,
Long, soggy, salty seaweed has been washed up on the sandy bay
And along with the seaweed, comes some brightly coloured shells,
Into the deep blue sea are turtles rolling around,
With their green backs shining up to the bright yellow sun,
Under the sand where the living dead lie,
Stella walks quickly to the end of the beach
And crumples the souls of the old ancient people . . .

Elisha Lyon
St Francis of Assisi Catholic Primary School, Skelmersdale

The City

As I walk through the city, I come upon
A dark, smoky, smelly alleyway.

I briskly walk through the alleyway
Looking left, right, up and down
Kicking the rubbish off the ground.

Out the alleyway, *phew!*
What surprise will come next?

I see houses - a mixed combination
Some are posh, some are poor
Some are clean, some are dirty
With the homeless sitting on the floor
What a weird little street.

Out of the street
And into the traffic.

I see posh cars zooming left and right
Double-decker buses
Stopping at the lights
White vans
Making lots of noise.

Finally, I reach my street
I dance and dance all the way
To my front door
I knock on the door
To my surprise, the dirty-looking door opens with a squeak
No one standing there
As I step inside the door
It dangerously slams shut
I'm *trapped!*
With something - but what could it be?

Darbie Barlow (11)
St Francis of Assisi Catholic Primary School, Skelmersdale

Unknown

The disturbing noise
The booming traffic
The loud laughter
It's too loud!
I can't hear myself think!
The large, loud, lively crowd won't stop shouting
Somebody make them stop!
I can see people eating
Peaceful babies quietly sleeping
Screeching cars loudly beeping
I can hear everything and everyone, but me.
But as I turn around
It's like I'm in a different dimension
I see nothing
Hear nothing
Feel nothing
I blink
I take another look
I see something bright
It's a flying light
But no one is holding it!
Is it a torch?
A candle?
What is it?
Where is it coming from?
Why is it flying around?
I blink again!
I see an enormous wooden house
A mansion!
It groans at me!
The house is alive!

Wiktoria Gerka (11)
St Francis of Assisi Catholic Primary School, Skelmersdale

Dead At Night

As the sun sets in the west,
A nearby house goes dark as the night.
In one of the rooms something isn't right!
There's an unmade bed in the corner of the room,
The old, wooden, creaky cupboard doors
Were open wide with clothes dragged out
And scattered all around!
The make-up set has been thrown everywhere,
The pink nail varnish spilt on the floor,
Broken glass crying sadly
And a lifeless body in a pool of blood,
The stab marks in the back of the girl
And the gunshot to her head
Are screaming in pain!
The footprints on the soft floor
Made of blood and shaped like a claw.
'We're watching you!'
It's horrifying!
You can hear her screaming, 'Stop!'
As she struggles to the phone.
Bang!
Once or twice
She haunts this house, she is the living dead!
This room hold a terrible secret and the question,
Who did this and why?

Saffron Ryan
St Francis of Assisi Catholic Primary School, Skelmersdale

Where Am I?

Where am I?
A moment ago I was in a lab
Now I'm cloaked in darkness
I can hear footsteps
Footsteps from another world
I wait for my eyes to adjust to the darkness
But they can't.
Suddenly . . .
The ground shakes like a loud thunderbolt
Crashing to the earth.
Will I die here?
Or be eaten by the darkness?
Boom!
The ground shakes again.
Boom!
Something is coming.
Boom!
Coming closer every second.
Boom!
Crash!
Something falls against the ground
Causing a tremendous earthquake
I can feel rocks tumbling from mountains
Where am I?

Callum Morgan Gary Henwood (11)
St Francis of Assisi Catholic Primary School, Skelmersdale

Untitled

Where am I?
Who am I?
What am I?
I am in a dusty, dark place,
Something strange running past me.

Animals here and there,
Ducks that are woolly white,
Trees that are grassy green,
Rats that are running all around my feet,
Branches that are crackling and falling off the trees,
Wolves that are eating,
Shooting noises from far away,
Bears that are growling,
Foxes that are dead,
Birds that are singing,
Where am I?
Who am I?
What am I?

Zoe Livesey (11)
St Francis of Assisi Catholic Primary School, Skelmersdale

Deserted Souls

The discomforting-looking house lay reluctantly on the hill,
The weary house looked at the working town below,
Sad laughter poured out of the old windows,
Eyes watched from the holes in the crooked curtains,
The antagonising eyes were not human,
The creepy eyes were not any mortal eyes,
The blank eyes were the tortured eyes of lost and forgotten souls,
The souls of the house's founders,
Who dedicated all to the once astonishing house
The house was built like a mansion,
But,
The deserted souls were locked in the house,
They were tortured in the house,
They are part of: the house!
They are cemented into the walls,
To haunt . . .
The house . . .
Forever!

Chris Haworth (10)
St Francis of Assisi Catholic Primary School, Skelmersdale

Storm!

Crash!
The storm is coming,
The golden sand blows across the wet shore,
As it starts to pour with rain,
The thunder groans, the lightning replies,
The last speck of daily sun glistens through the clouds,
The beach is empty,
The shells lay still on the seashore,
The brightly coloured beach ball rolls up and down the wet, soggy sand,
The rough water drags the sandcastles and lost seashells into its huge mouth,
The sea yawns loudly, forcing the waves to crash together and knock into the rough rocks,
The lifeguard flags blow as the wind gets heavier,
The puffy clouds are as black as new leather shoes,
The dark lightning runs across the sky,
The storm has arrived . . .

Lucy Hume (11)
St Francis of Assisi Catholic Primary School, Skelmersdale

The Black Widow

I am in a dark place,
I am cloaked in darkness,
A truck I see,
With cracked windows,
Like broken bones,
The blinding black widow,
I did not look!
Then suddenly . . .
Sad laughter!
Echoed through the dark alleyways,
Then something . . . moved!
Something small,
Not like me,
Something dangerous,
Could I dare to see?
I turned back to look
And what I saw was a . . . !

Liam Austin
St Francis of Assisi Catholic Primary School, Skelmersdale

He Makes Me Feel

He is . . .
Running as quickly as Usain Bolt running the 100 metres,
As quiet as a long-lost soul,
As tough as shiny, silvery metal,
He makes me feel inspired.

He is . . .
As shiny as a coin in the big, bright sun,
His hands are his deadliest weapon,
A yellow, spotty species,
His roar is as powerful as the world's strongest man,
He makes me feel strong,
His victims giggle with sad laughter,
Whoosh! He takes his prey.

He is . . .
A magnificent, wonderful cheetah,
He makes me feel awesome.

Thomas Wise (11)
St Francis of Assisi Catholic Primary School, Skelmersdale

Footprints . . .

Who is he . . . ?
An ice cream wrapper reluctantly rolls along the battered bay,
The wind mourns an echo of sad laughter,
As the roaring tide hesitates whether to go out or in,
Happy tears soften the crispy sand,
There are footprints . . . scattered across the crawling bay,
Footprints . . . *squelch!* As big as flippers,
Footprints . . . *squelch!* As deep as an ocean,
Are they footprints of a wild beast or footprints of a cat?
Maybe even the footprints of a suspicious man
Who died here four years ago . . . on this day!
Who is he . . . ?

Liam Murray
St Francis of Assisi Catholic Primary School, Skelmersdale

I Have A . . .

I have a rabbit that can play the flute,
I have a dog that can shoot,
Straight on target,
I have a kangaroo that can box,
I have a little red fox,
I have a bull frog that shops for me in the market.

I have a car that talks while it drives,
I have a wheelbarrow that can eat beehives,
I have a swing that brushes my mum's hair,
I have a stone that crawls and it is very rare.

I'm only joking,
I don't have any of these,
It's just fun to say, but I do have a cheese,
That will now do a disappearing act
Down my throat!

Gareth Smith (11)
St Paul's CE Primary School, Stalybridge

Up And Downs

A smile
A laugh

A cry
A frown

A murder in the dark

A groan
A moan

A giggle
A jiggle

Time to have a lark

A kiss
A hug

A kick
A bunch

A fight until the end

A yell
A shout

A sneak
A joke

They will drive you round the bend!

Rhiannon Stephenson (10)
St Paul's CE Primary School, Stalybridge

Illegal Immigrant Poem

(Inspired by a real-life experience)

I didn't mean to hurt you
I did it for myself
I also have some family
I really need to help.

I came here for a new start
England is the place
I know that some of your children
Think I'm a disgrace.

I came here for education
Also for a job
I really need a place to live
My old home makes me sob.

I really need some help
It was horrible in Sudan
I really need a better life
Or I will be an erratic man.

The police have put me in custody
I don't know what to do
Once again I would like to say
I'm sorry I frightened you.

Robbie Scott Hunter (11)
St Paul's CE Primary School, Stalybridge

Hugs

Hugs keep you warm,
Hugs keep you loving,
Hugs are as sweet as cherry pie,
Hugs are to show you love them,
Always love hugs!

Hugs show your loving side,
Hugs keep you loving everyone,
Hugs are as cuddly as teddy bears,
Hugs put love in your heart,
Always love hugs!

Hugs are meant to make you happy,
Hugs make you cheerful
Hugs are as soft as fluff,
Hugs mean the world to everyone,
Always love hugs!

Emma Louise Scanlan (11)
St Paul's CE Primary School, Stalybridge

Banana Pirates

Ahaar! Me hearties! We are the banana pirates!
We use our cutlasses to split you up, so the sharks can eat you up!
We wear eye patches and our hats so we can lure in the cats!
We have a parrot that squawks all day and copies everything we say!
We wear rags and we are proud to raise our flags!
We use our cannons to blow you up, we're always hungry so we eat up!
We attack our enemies for the gold that we use when we're old!
Ahaar! We like our treasure chests and we guard them from the bad pests!
We are yellow and we are strong and we always play along!
Ahaar! Me hearties! We are banana pirates!

Devon Bellamy & Luke Chisnall (10)
St Paul's CE Primary School, Stalybridge

The Forest Fire

The fire, which is getting high
Smoke is rising in the sky
Flames are burning all the logs
Scaring away all the dogs

All the trees are falling down
Fire gets out before it hits town
Lots of people scream and shout
The cats don't know what it's about

Now the forest is completely gone
All the trees are gone, except for one
Even though people are dead
Your children will be safe in bed.

George Smith (11)
St Paul's CE Primary School, Stalybridge

Eclipse

Dear Eclipse,
You are me
I am you
You are the best
I ever knew
With your frizzy black mane
I know your name
In my life you will remain
I will miss you
Lots of love!

Bethany Bailey (11)
St Paul's CE Primary School, Stalybridge

The Heart Of Me!

I'm a dancing dynamo
Fast in the swim lane
Love is my passion

The things I see
The things I do
All the things I care about

I'm still as I am
The essence of me
I'm as happy as I can be.

Ellie Goodyear (11)
St Paul's CE Primary School, Stalybridge

Biscuits

When I open the biscuit tin
Mainly there is nothing in
Chocolate fingers and custard creams
They're all in my brothers' dreams
Cheeky boys!

When I open the biscuit tin
I think everything's been put in the bin
They've been eaten so very quick
All this makes my fingers click
Cheeky boys!

When I open the biscuit tin
Mainly there is nothing in
I wonder who has eaten them all?
Maybe they're in the hall
Cheeky boys!

Nothing there . . .
Except crumbs!

Sarah Murray (9)
St William's RC (VA) Primary School, Trimdon

The Dragon

The dragon
With gleaming
Shiny
Scales
Like a star
Up
High

The dragon
Swift movements
As quick
As
Lightning

The dragon
Silent
But deadly
Never makes
A
Sound

The dragon
Contains
No fear
Will never
Back
Down

The dragon
Will
Fight no questions asked
The dragon
Now
Sleeps
For the night.

Blaize Marshall (10)
St William's RC (VA) Primary School, Trimdon

Under The Sea - Haikus

Fish scared as ever,
With a flash of tail are gone,
Into the deep sea.

Sharks terrifying,
Hungrily hunting for prey,
As all swim away.

Dolphins; squeaks and clacks,
Chattering away like friends,
Playing happily.

Eel, slippery,
Sliding through the deep blue sea,
An electric fish.

Swordfish wins the fight,
Battling for survival,
Always keeping safe.

Starfish; playing mate,
Star of the shimmering sea,
Always there for you.

Octopus out there,
Waving his eight legs at you,
Looking for his food.

Crabs that go *snap, snap,*
Walking sideways with his steps,
Ready for his lunch.

The biggest blue whale,
The biggest mammal on Earth,
Always there, ready.

Jellyfish gliding,
Through the clear water ready,
To sting anyone.

Natalie Bastiman (10)
St William's RC (VA) Primary School, Trimdon

We Will Rule The Rainbow Nation!

There is a buzz around the world,
Something is coming
And one day soon,
Three lions will roar
And take South Africa by storm!

We'll send the Slovenians running home!
We'll pass through the Algerians like they were made of foam!
And send the Americans back to the other side of the world!

Let's give it to the Germans,
Buckaroo the Brazilians back
And show the Argentineans how to counter attack!

This is a challenge we must face,
But with Rooney and Darren Bent,
We are bound to win the race!

We will rule the rainbow nation!
Forget the Spaniards and German superstars,
In the World Cup, there's only one fact known . . .
And that is . . .
'Football's coming home!'

William Reid (11)
St William's RC (VA) Primary School, Trimdon

We Are Going To Australia

I've packed my clothes
I've packed my toys
I've packed my bike
I've packed my TV

Woo-hoo!
I am going to Australia!

I've said bye to my mates
I've said bye to my nana
I've said bye to my grandad
I've said bye to the teachers

Woo-hoo!
I am going to Australia!

I've played with my friends
I've talked to the teachers
I've had my last moments
I've eaten my final family dinners

Woo-hoo!
We're going to Australia!

Dominic Howarth (8)
St William's RC (VA) Primary School, Trimdon

Mum Says

Mum says I am the best!
Mum says my brother's a pest!
Mum says you need less!
Mum says we need a guest!
Mum says have you done your test?
Mum says get off the new desk!
Mum says I am still the best!
That is what Mum says!

Lydia Sheldon (9)
St William's RC (VA) Primary School, Trimdon

Baby

There's a baby on its way,
If it's a girl we'll call her Fay.
We'll have to get a cot
And nappies for the little tot.

If it's a boy, we'll call him Bill,
I'll read to him 'Jack and Jill'.
We'll make him feel like a prince
And feed him veg and mince.

The baby is on its way,
Its birthday will be in May.
Screaming and crying,
The baby is arriving.

Wow! It's a girl,
Maybe we'll call her Pearl.
Her room is ready,
With a brand new teddy.

I love the new baby,
She'll be like me one day, maybe.

Shannon Louise Teresa Ferry (10)
St William's RC (VA) Primary School, Trimdon

The Earth

T he Earth
H ydrogen
E nergy

E lectricity
A ir
R ain
T rees
H eat.

Rebecca Elizabeth Dobson (10)
St William's RC (VA) Primary School, Trimdon

Our Planet

Earth is very small,
But it is time for protocol.
Factories and cars,
Make more carbon dioxide than on Mars.
Thanks to the trees, the oxygen will stay,
But all the lumber men will take them away.

Look in the river,
The sight makes me shiver.
All the nuclear waste,
That I have to face.
All the fish are dead
And the water is green and red.

Up at landfill sites,
They are infested with dust mites.
Old mattresses to a dust pan
And a rat that once quickly ran.
Rusty cars and a smelly stray cat
And inside, a soggy old hat.

Ethan Josef Mould (11)
St William's RC (VA) Primary School, Trimdon

Ball

Ball!
Cricket, catch
Tennis, basketball,
Baseball, dodgeball, netball,
American football,
Table tennis,
Football,
Ball!

Daniel Bastiman (9)
St William's RC (VA) Primary School, Trimdon

My Horse

I feel the warmth coming from my horse's muzzle,
Her eyes like shining diamonds
I brush her belly with a small body brush
I love the way she sometimes gives me a nudge
I comb her mane, not even a tangle
And her tail swishes in the wind
I put on her saddle and fasten her bridle
She's ready to ride, now I mount on her side.

With a click of my tongue and she's into a trot
I circle her round first just on the spot
I tap her on the belly and I am into a canter
Now the rest of the arena is flying past me so fast!
The lesson is over and I run up her stirrups
And loosen her girth
I put her in her stall and feed her a mint
She is my horse
My horse is my life.

Lauren Easton (11)
St William's RC (VA) Primary School, Trimdon

Broken Arm

B for brother
R for rip
O for *ouch!*
K for knife
E for extreme pain
N for naughty

A for agony
R for rash
M for moan

That's what pain feels like!

Ben Merrington (9)
St William's RC (VA) Primary School, Trimdon

Sweets

Some sweet, some sour
Mine are gone in half an hour
Sweets, sweets, I love the taste
My sweets never go to waste.

Rub my tummy, lick my lips
Afterwards lick my fingertips
Red, yellow, pink and green
Eating sweets I'll never stay lean.

Yes, I like my sweets a lot
I've loved them since I was in a cot
I'd say sweets are my favourite things
When I eat them, my head rings.

But who cares? Not really me
It's time to go for my tea
Where have all my sweets gone?
I was looking forward to my bonbon!

Katie Spellman (9)
St William's RC (VA) Primary School, Trimdon

My Dog Is . . .

My dog is a coward
My dog is a wimp
My dog is a whale
My dog is a blimp
My dog is a flower
My dog is a rose
I have to kiss her little wet nose.

Eavie Proffitt (9)
St William's RC (VA) Primary School, Trimdon

Will You Please . . .

Will you please sit down!
Will you please take a seat!
Will you please be quiet!
Will you please look neat!

Will you please clean your teeth!
Will you please wash your face!
Will you please find your shoe!
Will you please tie your lace!

Will you please get your clips!
Will you please get your locks!
Will you please get your coat!
Will you please get your socks!

Will you please hurry up!
Will you please come with me!
Look at the time,
It's nearly quarter-past nine!

Lucy Tate (9)
St William's RC (VA) Primary School, Trimdon

Polly Pocket

Polly Pocket picked some peas
The peas were very pink
Perfectly Polly picked a prickly pineapple
From the purple pavement
Polly politely placed the prickly pineapple
The pink peas and some perfumed peaches
Into her perfect pocket.

Callum Atkinson (9)
St William's RC (VA) Primary School, Trimdon

Paddy

My dog is called Paddy
He acts to be quite tough
But really when he barks and growls
Really he's a wuss

Paddy

Sitting by the window
Playing with his toys
Waiting for his friends
Mostly they're all boys

Paddy

Running, sprinting, jogging
Until he is puffed out
Trying to find his chew
Wandering about

Paddy!

Jade Oakes (10)
St William's RC (VA) Primary School, Trimdon

The Earth Poem

E arth is a tranquil planet and peaceful world
A nimals live here in harmony
R ivers run through the land
T hunder and lightning in the sky
H undreds of millions of people live on Earth.

Jack Foote (9)
St William's RC (VA) Primary School, Trimdon

Hot Chocolate

```
        The                  And
Very                    You
    Hot                     Drink
        Steam                   It
        Rises                   From
            Up                      A cup
```
It's silky, milky, hot and smooth,
It's drippy, slippy, brown and tasty,
Cocoa powder, hot water and milk
It's so delicious and the nice heat is vicious
You so, so want to consume   it
You so, so want to drink   it
Delicious, scrumptious, frothy and it's brothy
Hot chocolate is the best
If you have not tried it
Take the taste test!

Eddie Reid (9)
St William's RC (VA) Primary School, Trimdon

Silly Sisters

Silly Sally and Silly Sue
Live together in a zoo
Silly zoo, Silly Sally, Silly Sue
And so are you
Silly Sally and Silly Sue
They are arguing over you
They are arguing over you
Because Silly Sally is jealous of Sue
Silly Sally said to Sue
He will never ever love you
Silly Sally and Silly Sue
Live together in a zoo!

Aleysha Oakes (10)
St William's RC (VA) Primary School, Trimdon

Pirates, Pirates, Pirates

Pirates, pirates, pirates
Angry, aggressive, awful pirates
Miserable, monstrous, mischievous pirates
Pirates, pirates, pirates

Daft, dull, dangerous pirates
Stupid, silly, smelly pirates
Pirates, pirates, pirates

Pirates, pirates, pirates
Horrible, hideous, horrid pirates
Nasty, naughty, needy pirates
Pirates, pirates, pirates!

Jake Fishburn (9)
Spennithorne CE Primary School, Spennithorne

Meet The Pirates

These are the most idiotic pirates
Pirate Bob who has a big gob
Pirate Tom who has a bomb
Pirate Ella who has an umbrella
Pirate Tim who likes to swim
Pirate Will who likes to drill
These are the most stupid pirates!

Jamie Harrington (8)
Spennithorne CE Primary School, Spennithorne

The News: Hens

Here is the news
Of a clever hen
Of a clever hen
That is the news

The hen got caught
And then it was bought

It fluttered on the farmyard gate
And it had to wait

It walked in its pen
With two other hens

It came out in fog
And it sank in a bog

It came out when sunny
And got a little money

It came out in the wind
And got in a spin

But (I'm happy to say)
In a frost
Another hen got lost.

Lauren Fall (9)
Spennithorne CE Primary School, Spennithorne

Pirates

Pirates, pirates, pirates
Cool, clumsy, keen pirates
Determined, dull, daft pirates
Pirates, pirates, pirates

Pirates, pirates, pirates
Ruthless, rough, rigid pirates
Plump, popular, parrot pirates
Pirates, pirates, pirates

Pirates, pirates, pirates
Howling, hollering, happy pirates
Ferocious, fiery, funny pirates
Pirates, pirates, pirates

Pirates, pirates, pirates
Mucky, mean, marvellous pirates
Angry, amber, awful pirates
Pirates, pirates, pirates

Pirates, pirates, pirates
Yucky, yellow, young pirates
Silly, superstitious, surprising pirates
Pirates, pirates, pirates.

Maggie Manning (9)
Spennithorne CE Primary School, Spennithorne

Pirates, Pirates, Pirates

Funny, fat, fragrant pirates
Cross, cold, damp pirates
Pirates, pirates, pirates.

Pirates, pirates, pirates
Jumping, jam, jelly pirates
Tiny, terrible, tubby pirates.

Pirates, pirates, pirates
Happy, handsome, horrible pirates
Silly, shiny, slinky pirates.

Pirates, pirates, pirates
Pooey, pink, pokey pirates
Big, bad, blue pirates.

Pirates, pirates, pirates
Okay, old, odour-whiffy pirates
Daft, dull, dumb pirates
Pirates, pirates, pirates!

Tom Partridge (9)
Spennithorne CE Primary School, Spennithorne

Meet The Pirates

Aboard a rocky pirate ship in the middle of the sea
Are a funny group of pirates who are as silly as can be
Pirate Tim who likes to swim
Pirate Bob eats with his gob
Pirate Dan is a man
Pirate Ben is ten
Pirate Hay has to pay
Pirate Cat has a hat
Pirate Gam has a mam
They are a funny group of pirates!

Emily Wilson (8)
Spennithorne CE Primary School, Spennithorne

Pirates, pirates, pirates

Pirates, pirates, pirates
Angry, awful, aggressive pirates
Dumb, dangerous, daring pirates
Pirates, pirates, pirates

Pirates, pirates, pirates
Scary, silly, smelly pirates
Huge, horrible, hideous pirates
Pirates, pirates, pirates

Pirates, pirates, pirates
Mischievous, mad, miniscule pirates
Nasty, naughty, needy pirates
Pirates, pirates, pirates!

Jack Harry Tait (9)
Spennithorne CE Primary School, Spennithorne

Meet The Pirates

Aboard a rocky pirate ship in the middle of the sea
Are a funny group of pirates who are as useless as can be

There's Pirate Bob who has a big gob
Pirate Tim who likes to swim
Pirate Cameron who's afraid of the cannon
Pirate Matt who wears a hat
Pirate Ella who has an umbrella
Pirate Tom who has a big bomb
Pirate Ruth who lost a tooth
Pirate Jake who likes to bake
Pirate Polly who has a dolly.

George Leathley (9)
Spennithorne CE Primary School, Spennithorne

The News

Here is the news
About a beautiful flower
About a beautiful flower
That was the news

The pigeon flew by with a pie
A stork flew by to get a cork
(Sad to say)
It got stood on, a petal blew away
Here is the news
About a beautiful flower
About a beautiful flower.

Bethany Harrington (8)
Spennithorne CE Primary School, Spennithorne

Meet The Stupid Pirate Pack

Floating across the sea are pirates drinking tea
They are the most stupid pirates there can be
There's Pirate Hazel who eats basil
Pirate Rebecca May who sleeps in a barrel of hay
Pirate Jo-Anne who sleeps in a pan
Pirate Mars who eats chocolate bars
Pirate Paint who is a saint
Pirate Pat who sleeps on a cat
And Pirate James who uses canes!

Olivia Eyre (7)
Spennithorne CE Primary School, Spennithorne

Meet The Pirates

Aboard a rocky pirate ship in the middle of the sea
Are a funny group of pirates who are as funny as can be
Pirate Ruth who has lost a tooth
Pirate Ella who has an umbrella
Pirate Tom who is scared of a bomb
Pirate Daniel who has a spaniel
Pirate Jake who likes to rake
Pirate Molly who has a dolly
Who are as funny as can be!

Ruth Metcalfe (9)
Spennithorne CE Primary School, Spennithorne

Meet The Pirates

Aboard a rocky pirate ship in the middle of the sea
Are a funny group of pirates who are as useless as can be

There's Pirate Ben who likes to build a den
Pirate Rex who likes T-rex
Pirate Luke who steals loot
Pirate Love who likes doves
Pirate Dip who likes to nip
Pirate Jon who likes bombs.

Matthew Heinze (9)
Spennithorne CE Primary School, Spennithorne

The Worst Pirates In The World

Pirate Daniel that had a spaniel
Pirate Tom that had a bomb
Pirate Ruth that had one tooth
Pirate Bill that liked to swill
Pirate Will that liked to kill
Pirate Bob that had a big gob
Pirate Sam that liked a ram
As silly as can be!

William Cooper (8)
Spennithorne CE Primary School, Spennithorne

Mixed Emotions

Some days you're happy
Some days you're sad
Some days you're stupid
Some days you're bad
Some days you're crazy
Some days you're mad

Some days you're just . . .

Lewis Moorcroft (10)
Stradbroke Primary School, Sheffield

In The Woods

On a gloomy night
With all fright
I can hear trees coming alive.

I can't see anything
Pitch-black.

I can sense a presence in the air
My heart is beating as fast as possible.

Burnt ashes in the deadly air
Signs of terror
Run down my unconscious spine.

Boiling volcanoes
Lava racing down high mountains
Coming to smother me
I have no choice . . .
I must run down this mysterious, gloomy way.

Footsteps getting louder
I don't know what to do.

Footsteps getting closer . . .
In these wild, wild woods.

Isobel Vaughan (10)
Stradbroke Primary School, Sheffield

Fear

The colour of the black sky
It smells like Medusa's armpits
Sweaty socks
I feel like I've just woken up from the dead
Its claws are as sharp as a vampire's teeth
The footsteps are like a car's brakes.

Aaron Shaw & Connor Walsh (10)
Stradbroke Primary School, Sheffield

Love Is In The Air

As I pass him, my heart skips a beat
I can do nothing but stare
His eyes sparkle and his hair is silky and soft
My body goes all weak
And my belly feels like jelly

Years later, wedding bells ring
My father walks me down the aisle
I am in my white, pretty wedding dress
Flowers surround me
And smiles spread like a roaring fire

Years pass again
A baby is born
My husband gives me a warm, kind look
It's a baby girl
She is called Alice

All this started with the feeling of love.

Libby Hines (10)
Stradbroke Primary School, Sheffield

Food Poem

Eggs and bacon,
Cheese and chips,
Spaghetti Bolognese
Crunch, crunch, crunch!

Crisps and chocolate,
Lemonade and Coke,
Chicken and cookies,
Chew, chew, chew!

Sausage rolls and cabbage
What? Never any veg!

Olivia Clarke (9)
Stradbroke Primary School, Sheffield

Sad Bumps

Ohh, ow! Bumped my head,
Now my skull is getting red.

Ouch, ooh! Scratched my knees,
Urgh! It tastes like mouldy cheese.

Ouch, ow! Stubbed my toe,
It smells like a murdered crow.

Ooh, ow! Banged my nose,
It's stretched out like a long red hose.

Ouch, ooh! Broke my nook,
It sounds like a woodpecker with its peck.

Ow, ouch! I've been stung,
It looks like a bruise and piles of dung.

Life isn't fair at all!

Charlie Bower (10)
Stradbroke Primary School, Sheffield

Secrets

No time to dream and lie,
Just joined as a spy,
Look what I just found . . .
Super gadgets all around!
A super whip,
A killer stick,
No dreams,
No lies,
I chose this life,
But why . . . ?

Joshua Kelly (9)
Stradbroke Primary School, Sheffield

Love

Light, ruby-red, shining
As light as a red ruby ring
It tastes like melting, velvety chocolate
Melting in your mouth
Fresh green grass
An angel playing a harp
Drifting you off to sleep
A beating heart
Romance in the dark
Dancing around with love in your heart.

Ebony Wilson, Amber Bowie (10) & Adam Marples (9)
Stradbroke Primary School, Sheffield

Happy

Shining rainbow in the deep blue sky
Happiness tastes like fresh strawberries covered in chocolate sauce
Happiness is yellow shimmering in the sun
As green as freshly grown grass
Pink as a jolly pig
Freshly picked red roses
Feathers on a chicken
Music playing on a merry-go-round
Like finding a twenty pound note on the floor
Happy!

Holly Liversidge & Georgia Greaves (10)
Stradbroke Primary School, Sheffield

Loneliness

Empty streets all around
No one but myself
The echoing of my own voice
In a damp, gloomy alleyway
Like a cold, empty hand touching me constantly
Making chills creep down my spine
In the distance I see a grey mist
Sneaking closer and closer until . . .
A tear rolls down my cheek
Loneliness.

Lucy Birch (10) & Kady Shepley (9)
Stradbroke Primary School, Sheffield

The Creepy Hall

I walk on my own
Down the dark, creepy hall
I heard a little girl calling me
I walk towards the sound
Songs float down the hall
She's singing
Making me scared

Who is she?
What does she want?

Charlotte Mellor (10)
Stradbroke Primary School, Sheffield

Silence

Silence feels like rain pouring down on a miserable day
Silence looks like dark, gloomy cave on a slippery day
Silence reminds me of a ghost in a haunted house
Silence is the colour of pitch-black and grey clouds
Silence tastes like lemon squeezed into my mouth
Silence smells like a heartbroken day
Silence sounds like an empty room.

Maisie Marriott (8)
Stradbroke Primary School, Sheffield

I'm All Alone

Dark streets
Filled with ghosts
From the past
I'm the only survivor
I'm the only human on Earth
All the rest of the humans
Will never
Come
Back . . .

Joshua Hirst & Corben Timms (10)
Stradbroke Primary School, Sheffield

Love

Love tastes like white sugar
Love looks like a red heart in the sky
Love feels like an enormous cuddle
Love reminds me of my mum and dad getting married
Love is the colour red
Love sounds like birds.

Curtis Emmingham (8)
Stradbroke Primary School, Sheffield

Love

Love feels like a big hug from your family
Love tastes like pink ice cream
Love is brown, like chocolate
Love reminds me of my family when I am sad
Love smells like a flower that has fallen off a tree
Love sounds like the birds singing a song
Love looks like a man and woman having their picture taken.

Alicia Beniston (7)
Stradbroke Primary School, Sheffield

Mr Lonely

It feels like I'm the only one left in the world
I feel like I'm trapped in a dark, empty room
Being lonely tastes like milk gone bad
It's going to haunt me forever
It echoes in my ear
I just want it to stop!

Leighann Sharpe & Natalie Hawkins (10)
Stradbroke Primary School, Sheffield

Fury

Steaming down the corridor
Fed-up
Bored with life
Blood boiling as hot as fire
Marching like a soldier
On my way to war.

Jayden Lee Moat (10)
Stradbroke Primary School, Sheffield

Silence

Silence feels like a dark, gloomy cave
Silence feels like the moon going black
Silence is like a blackout
Silence tastes like a rotten piece of bacon
Silence reminds me of my little brother in his room, asleep in bed
Silence smells like a wet, stinky cave.

Adam Holmshaw (8)
Stradbroke Primary School, Sheffield

Dan The Man

Stomping down the stairs
Without going to the fair
Dan feels very angry
As his friends are going there
He gets furious
As he smashes his mum's jewellery.

Shelby Emmingham (10)
Stradbroke Primary School, Sheffield

Excited

Fresh, sweet cream just out of the fridge
Golden yellow as bright as the sun
People screaming with joy and racing around the fair
A bowl of melted chocolate, so great and creamy
A cute baby puppy, so sweet and loveable
It makes you feel like it's Christmas morning every day.

Abbigail Beniston & Andrew Gregory (10)
Stradbroke Primary School, Sheffield

Love

Love feels like a big hug
Love tastes like a sweet lollipop
Love looks like me and my mum hugging
Love smells like chocolate
Love reminds me of me playing with my sister
Love is the colour pink, like my mum's lips.

Kelsey Bellamy (7)
Stradbroke Primary School, Sheffield

Happiness

Happiness feels like a hug
Happiness is when you laugh
Happiness is the colour light blue
Happiness looks like my dad and me laughing
Happiness reminds me of my mum.

Caiden Smith (7)
Stradbroke Primary School, Sheffield

Love

Love is my mum's pink lips kissing me
Love smells like my dad's armpits when he is hugging me
Love reminds me of my mum hugging me
Love reminds me of my family hugging and kissing me
Love smells like my mum's perfume.

Paige Pickering (7)
Stradbroke Primary School, Sheffield

Happiness

Happiness feels like getting a new soft pet
Happiness reminds me of my friends playing with me
Happiness smells like a sweet lollipop
Happiness looks like smiling faces in a park
Happiness is bright pink, like my mum's lips.

Kathryn Robinson (8)
Stradbroke Primary School, Sheffield

Fun

Fun looks like a toddler going down a slide
Fun sounds like kids screaming with excitement
Fun smells of the sea with lots of children bouncing on the waves
Fun reminds me of when we go to parties
Fun is like a family in the paddling pool, getting brown.

Georgia Johnston (8)
Stradbroke Primary School, Sheffield

Love

Love is blue like the sky
Love feels like a red heart
Love reminds me of a hug
Love sounds like birds singing.

Tommy Cooke (8)
Stradbroke Primary School, Sheffield

Sad

Sad and lonely on the street
No money to buy stuff to eat
No friends, it's a gloomy black sky
Nothing to do at all . . .

Georgie Samantha Jackson (10)
Stradbroke Primary School, Sheffield

Fun

Fun feels like a heart of gold
Fun looks like eating chocolate chip cake
Fun smells like pizza
Fun reminds me of my mum giving me a kiss.

Kyle Joseph Haig (8)
Stradbroke Primary School, Sheffield

Shark

Blood drinker
Best swimmer
Man eater
Blue colour
Teeth sharper than a razor
Best hider
Sharp swimmer
He is a biter
Tail swisher
Fish hunter
High jumper
Fish eater.

Richard Michael Ireland (8)
The Park Primary School, Runcorn

Sharks

Fast swimmer
Good eater
Camouflaged in water
Grey hunter
Teeth like razors
Waving tails very fast.

Lee May (8)
The Park Primary School, Runcorn

Let Him Live A Normal Life!

How dare they treat the poor creature like this!
I can see the agony
The sadness
Through his face
His eyes were all bloodshot
Barely open and lost-looking
I mean, why?
Why put sharp metal through his nose?
Just to pull him round like a fluff ball on string
What's the world turning to these days?
How would their owners feel to be treated this way?
What major crime has the bear done wrong?
He's got a big hole through his nose
And he's being dragged around like a puppet!
Nobody laughs!
We all just find it appalling
The evil owner knows that too!
But they never give it up
Just let the poor creature live a normal life!

Alice Routledge (11)
Walsden St Peter's CE Primary School, Todmorden

Please Help The Fool

I'm a fool!
I've got no food, no water
My skin
My skin is damaged, cut and scratched
My owner doesn't have enough money to care for me properly
My hooves are worn down
I look a fool!

People stare . . .
What's to stare at?
I'm ugly, disgusting
I can't take another step further
It hurts
A whole lot of fun this is!
I need rest, sleep
Please?
I feel like a fool
Please help the fool!

Amy Cupac (11)
Walsden St Peter's CE Primary School, Todmorden

Time To Die

Why am I going to die
Beneath this tribal net?
From day to day when not in the net,
The exhaust fumes suffocate me.

At time to time, I get distressed,
With these ugly-looking aliens,
They make my life Hell,
It's like I'm living in a cell.

Jack Cryer (11)
Walsden St Peter's CE Primary School, Todmorden

Harmless

I'm dying, dying
I don't know what to do
I'm bleeding inside
I need you!

The harmless creature
Left all alone
That's me, that is
I just want to go home.

I have to run now!
Before I get caught
They're driving after me
I have to abort.

I might give myself in
After all, I'm rubbish
That's what they called me
They traded me for a fish!

Sara Power (10)
Walsden St Peter's CE Primary School, Todmorden

The Dreading Soul

The nets fall in
The sea
Swirling and curling
Making ripples on
The ocean surface
Blocking the motion
Of the shark
Trying to mark
The dreading soul
Lending and ending
The life by force.

Adam Georgiou (10)
Walsden St Peter's CE Primary School, Todmorden

The Grey Whale!

I'm here,
Because,
I love whales,
I love watching whales,
But I didn't expect to see this.

The anger,
The frustration,
It's too much,
I can't help the dying beast.

So what can I do?
I can't just stand here in shock
Watching the gentle giant's skin rip and slide off
Just looking in the poor creature's eyes,
You can see agony
And loneliness.

Ria Montgomery (11)
Walsden St Peter's CE Primary School, Todmorden

Whale

Why, oh, why, is my precious life ending?
My tears drop silently, into the red, deadly sea
Red, red with my own blood
The sharp arrow pierces my precious skin
I am starting to rise from the sea
Immediately I pass away
Now something is happening to me
But I don't know what.

Joe Wright (11)
Walsden St Peter's CE Primary School, Todmorden

Frustration

The anger,
The frustration,
I'm helpless here!
All they want is my fat!

As the sharp metal
Pierces my skin,
More and more
Blood pours out.

I am brought to the surface,
I cannot help myself,
Can anyone help me?
Please! Please! Please!

Katie Skowron (11)
Walsden St Peter's CE Primary School, Todmorden

Red Raindrops

I twist and turn
The snow leopard is trapped
In a pit
My new house

Spots of my blood
Paint the snow
Like red raindrops
Making wavy patterns

I hear them
Sounds from above
It won't be long
Before my fur and flesh are torn . . .

Rhys Moores (10)
Walsden St Peter's CE Primary School, Todmorden

Followed By Bees

I'm a monkey in the trees,
Getting followed by bees,
I hide behind hollowed trees,
When the branch fell on my head,
I thought I was dead,
That's how I got the massive lump,
Now I'm a grumpy monkey.

Josh Hird (10)
Walsden St Peter's CE Primary School, Todmorden

Fun

What does it feel like?
It feels like a bright red clown nose.

What does it remind you of?
A large circus.

What colour is it?
Bright orange.

What does it smell like?
A big red flower.

What does it taste like?
A huge cream pie.

What does it sound like?
People laughing.

What does it look like?
People on a trapeze.

Brydon Kenney (9)
Woodhouse Community Primary School, Bishop Auckland

Peace

What does it sound like?
Birds singing sweetly in the trees.

What does it look like?
People saying very nice things to each other.

What does it feel like?
Making a chocolate cake for tea.

What does it remind you of?
People having a quiet drink.

What colour is it?
Light blue like the sea.

What does it smell like?
Roses in the garden.

What does it taste like?
Lovely fresh air.

Kamran Howard (8)
Woodhouse Community Primary School, Bishop Auckland

Football

David Beckham
Cristiano Ronaldo
All I know is they are good at it.

He kicks the ball
It's a goal!

But what I know is
I like them all
They have been
Playing for years.

Bethany Smirthwaite (10)
Woodhouse Community Primary School, Bishop Auckland

Fun

What does it look like?
Clowns balancing from a 10 foot rope.

What does it remind you of?
The fast rides at Legoland.

What does it sound like?
Children shouting and screaming.

What does it taste like?
Yummy candyfloss.

What does it smell like?
Prawns on the beach.

What colour is it?
Blue, like the sea.

What does it feel like?
A ripe pomegranate.

Sean McGrady (8)
Woodhouse Community Primary School, Bishop Auckland

Funny Poems

I hate a bully
With a big belly
When I stand up to him
I just call him smelly

Danger can happen
At the wink of an eye
When I fall asleep
Kaboom! Goodbye!

Aaron Bailey (10)
Woodhouse Community Primary School, Bishop Auckland

The Seaside

Cold splash
Quite nice
Summer's day
Hot clash
Big waves
Get wet
People swimming
Families chatting
Children playing
Starting to rain
Everyone is going
Tide coming in.

Courtney Louise Hopps (11)
Woodhouse Community Primary School, Bishop Auckland

Cars

Some long
Some short
Amphibious and green
Tall
Small
Colourful
Dull
All I know is that they are cars!

Ashley Cumberland (10)
Woodhouse Community Primary School, Bishop Auckland

Love

What does it smell of?
Red roses from the florist's.

What colour is it?
Like a red beating heart.

What does it feel like?
Someone who is happy.

What does it look like?
Your parents.

What does it remind you off?
Holidays with my family.

What does it taste like?
Red cherry lips.

What does it sound like?
Listening to the stereo.

Chloe Pattison (8)
Woodhouse Community Primary School, Bishop Auckland

Simpson's Poetry

Mister Burns is grumpy and old
And Smithers does what he's told
Santa's Little Helper dreams of a sheep
That can jump a metre
Maggie's a baby who carries a gun
When she shoots you, she says it's for fun!

Lee Anderson (11)
Woodhouse Community Primary School, Bishop Auckland

Sadness

What does it smell of?
Like tears when you are crying.

What colour is it?
Deep blue, like the sea.

What does it feel like?
An awful rainy day.

What does it feel like?
Very bad.

What does it remind you of?
God crying.

What does it sound like?
Someone crying.

What does it taste like?
The salty water of tears.

Kieran Pattison (9)
Woodhouse Community Primary School, Bishop Auckland

Young Writers Information

We hope you have enjoyed reading this book - and that you will continue to enjoy it in the coming years.

If you like reading and writing poetry drop us a line, or give us a call, and we'll send you a free information pack.

Alternatively if you would like to order further copies of this book or any of our other titles, then please give us a call or log onto our website at www.youngwriters.co.uk

A platform for your poetry!

Young Writers Information
Remus House
Coltsfoot Drive
Peterborough
PE2 9JX
(01733) 890066

Get in touch!